PEEL YOUR OWN ONION

WORKSHOP PARTICIPANT'S WORKBOOK

by

DAVID C. PROSSER

Copyright © 1979 by David C. Prosser

All rights reserved. No part of this publication may be reproduced, stored in a retrieval system, or transmitted in any form or by any means, electronic, mechanical, photocopying, recording, or otherwise without the prior written permission of the author, his assigns, or Personal Planning Programs, Inc.

Personal Planning Programs, Inc.
Suite 222
6550 York Avenue South
Edina, Minnesota 55435

INTRODUCTION TO THE PEEL YOUR
OWN ONION WORKSHOP

Welcome to the Peel Your Own Onion Workshop! My name is David Prosser.

You are about to participate in a unique life growth experience in which you learn to plan and manage your life like a successful small business. You'll learn a personal planning process that has literally changed my life and the lives of several hundreds of other men and women. Like peeling onions, you'll be able to peel away one layer or challenge in your life at a time. And with each successive layer, you'll learn more about yourself, more about what you're aiming for, and how to achieve it.

Is it really possible to manage your life like a successful small business? I believe it is! Let me tell you how I know this to be true.

For the past twenty-five years, I have managed several successful small businesses and functioned as a management consultant to others. Over a period of almost ten years, I worked on developing a comprehensive business planning process unlike any that existed at that time. I helped a number of organizations apply this planning process to their business enterprises. In many cases, the results exceeded expectations. Using my planning system, one manufacturer increased sales and profits 400% in four years. A public relations firm expanded from two full-time employees to eleven in nine months, with sales and profits to match. A research and development laboratory in another business reduced by 50% the amount of time needed to get its new products to market.

Such dynamic results led me to think: "Why can't the techniques of running a successful business be used to help individuals improve the effectiveness of their lives? Of my life?"

It was then that I began to look at my life as a small business - I, Incorporated. I analyzed my life as I would a business, looking carefully at my functions, my goals, and the problems I faced at that time. Then I applied the planning system I had used so successfully in my professional work to my personal life. As a result, the problems I faced at the time gave way to solutions. My wife and I, after spending months together working on our problems with a marriage counselor, began to see our relationship improve. We successfully "peeled the onion," and the reward has been a happier, more meaningful relationship in our marriage.

CONTENTS

	Page
Introduction to the Peel Your Own Onion Workshop	1
Introduction to the Peel Your Own Onion Workbook	6
Session 1: Introduction to Onion Peeling	8
Session 2: Starting with the Aha! Chart	19
Session 3: Identifying Your Needs	33
Session 4: Priority Setting	44
Session 5: Introduction to the Planning Process	59
Session 6: Taking Your Environment Into Account	70
Session 7: Your Action Plan	79
Session 8: Analyzing and Auditing Your Action Plan	91
Session 9: The Onion Peeler's Convention	129
Peeling More Layers	132

Soon after, I began sharing my personal planning process with others. In workshops, I taught the process to people from all walks of life and discovered that it is <u>universally applicable</u> to almost any life situation! A hard-driving businessman, using my planning process, learned to relax and enrich his life with new friendships. A divorced woman stepped out of her previously limited life style and discovered new avenues to a more rewarding social life. A housewife learned to fulfill her up-to-now neglected self-esteem needs by pursuing a career.

Now I want to share what I have learned with you. I am confident that you, too, can learn to plan and manage your life like a successful small business and become happier and more productive. I can't teach you how to improve your marriage, solve career problems, or become a millionaire. But I can help you learn a natural planning process that will send you along the road to achieving your personal goals. And like me, I think you'll find peeling onions a very rewarding occupation!

David C. Rosser

GOALS OF THE PEEL YOUR OWN ONION WORKSHOP

The ultimate goal of the Peel Your Own Onion Workshop is to help you learn the "onion-peeling process" and apply it to a problem you are facing now. Specifically, the workshop is designed to help you:

1. Learn to identify your personal needs and which needs are not being satisfied now.

2. Use priority setting to identify and deal with the most important need-related problem in your life.

3. Use my natural planning process to work on the problem you have selected.

4. Learn to monitor your progress in solving your problem and make adjustments in your plans as needed.

Upon completing the workshop, you will have a clear cut plan for resolving the problem you have selected, and you will have taken your first steps towards putting your plan into action. You will have started your own onion peeling process. And, once your first layer or problem is peeled, you'll have all the information and techniques you need to go on peeling still more layers of your onion. All the while, you will be learning more about yourself and getting closer to achieving your goals in life.

HOW THE WORKSHOP OPERATES

The Peel Your Own Onion Workshop consists of a number of sessions in which you and a small group of other workshop participants learn and use the onion-peeling process. A workshop facilitator will conduct the sessions and assist you in your onion-peeling. But, ultimately, it is _you_ who will do the peeling, because only you have the personal information and understanding to deal with your own issues, problems and goals effectively!

The workshop employs a number of learning techniques designed to help you quickly learn and effectively use the onion-peeling process. You'll be hearing mini-lectures given by your workshop facilitator, and you'll be participating in small group discussions and exercises. Most importantly, you will be working either individually or with others through each step of the onion-peeling process as it applies to the problem you've selected.

You already have received the kit of materials you'll be using throughout the workshop. There are two books in the kit. <u>Peel Your Own Onion</u> is a textbook I have written to give you a detailed understanding of the onion-peeling process. There will be regular reading assignments in this book, so be prepared to do a little homework! The book you are reading now, <u>The Peel Your Own Onion Workshop Participant's Workbook</u>, contains a number of activities you'll be doing either during the workshop sessions or at home. In this book, you'll be working through each step of the onion process, making notes on what you are learning and writing your plans for resolving the problem you have chosen to work on. In addition, several key charts shown in the text are included in the kit as convenient aids in working through the onion peeling process.

<u>YOUR ROLE IN THE WORKSHOP</u>

Your primary role is to be "Your Own Onion Peeler." As I said earlier, only you have the personal information and self-understanding to select the problem that is most important to you and to plan how to resolve it in a way that's meaningful to you. The workshop facilitator and the other workshop participants may offer you helpful information and critiques of your progress through the process, but <u>you</u> are the onion-peeling expert with regard to your personal issues, problems, and goals in life!

On the other hand, you'll also be assuming the role of "Onion-Peeling Helper" to the other participants throughout the workshop. There will be many activities in which participants will be sharing with you their thinking and plans with regard to the problems they are peeling. You will be in a position to offer them insightful comments and information, but always with the awareness that each person is ultimately his or her own Onion Peeler. I think you'll find this role a rewarding one to fulfill as you watch each of the other participants work successfully through the various stages of the onion-peeling process! You may even find that you are peeling very similar onion layers!

<u>YOUR WORKSHOP FACILITATOR'S ROLE</u>

Your workshop facilitator is here to guide you through the onion peeling process. He or she will be giving mini-lectures or talks on each step of the process and will answer any questions that you may have. Your facilitator will also be assisting in the small group discussions and exercises. As a fellow onion-peeler, he or she also may be sharing with you his or her own past or current onion-peeling projects.

One point to keep in mind about the facilitator's role in the workshop is that it is not as a psychological counselor or therapist. Unless your facilitator is a trained psychologist, he or she cannot offer you a professional opinion about "why" you feel the way you do or have the problems you currently face. The facilitator can, however, ask you questions that will help _you_ explore your needs, identify problems, and plan how to resolve them. He or she is primarily a "facilitator," available to assist you as you successfully peel your own onion and move closer to achieving your personal goals in life.

BENEFITS OF THE PEEL YOUR OWN ONION WORKSHOP

Workshops can be an effective way of helping people learn new information. The Peel Your Own Onion Workshop, however, can do a whole lot more than that. When I first began conducting this workshop, I was struck by the powerful dynamics of people interacting with one another and learning together as they proceeded through the onion-peeling process.

The benefits they derived were immediate and productive. Many persons found that by working with and listening to other workshop participants, they were better able to perceive and understand their own needs and problems. When they shared their onion-peeling plans with other workshop participants, they found the constructive comments coming their way of inestimable help in fine-tuning their plans. They also discovered that the positive support of the group was a great stimulus in motivating them to put their plans into action and follow through with them.

These are the benefits the Peel Your Own Onion Workshop offers you today. As a workshop facilitator and veteran onion-peeler myself, I have seen hundreds of men and women gain from these benefits, starting with the very first workshop session. I am confident that you will, as well!

INTRODUCTION TO THE PEEL YOUR OWN
ONION WORKBOOK

THE PURPOSE OF THE WORKBOOK

This workbook is designed to help you work through each step of the onion-peeling process. It is meant for your use alone, so that you can feel free to record in it whatever personal information you wish. You will be using the workbook both during the workshop sessions and at home.

THE CONTENTS OF THE WORKBOOK

The workbook consists of nine sections corresponding to the nine major sessions of the workshop. Each section contains:

1. Goals of the session

    Upon completing the session, you will have accomplished these goals.

2. Directions for workshop activities

    These directions are for such activities as small group discussions and exercises.

3. Note-taking space

    You may wish to write notes during the facilitator's talks, small group discussions, or when you are reading the textbook at home.

4. Specific onion-peeling activities

    These activities contain questions that will help you write down your thoughts, feelings, and specific plans as you proceed through the onion-peeling process during the workshop.

5. Journal assignments

    These are "homework" assignments consisting of questions that will help you reflect on what you have learned so far in the onion-peeling process and how you are progressing. The extent to which you do these assignments will depend on the format of the workshop in which you are participating.

Before your last workshop session, you will have several weeks to work on your personal onion peeling plan. At the end of this book are some <u>daily progress and auditing charts</u> that will help you closely monitor and record your progress in achieving your plan.

HOW TO GET THE MOST FROM THIS WORKBOOK

First, look over the book by paging briefly through it. This will give you a feeling for what the workshop will be like and what will be discussed.

Second, remember always to bring this book with you to the workshop sessions. You'll be using it in a number of activities, and you'll want to write notes in it frequently.

Third, make it a habit to actually write in the workbook, rather than just thinking about your answers to journal questions, exercises, small group discussion topics, etc. Learning specialists point out that we only learn when we <u>process</u> information and thus make it our own. Writing the information down in your own words is one very good way of processing this information!

Fourth, do <u>all</u> the activities presented in the workbook. They are designed to help you learn and apply the onion peeling process in the most effective way possible.

Fifth, when you have successfully completed your plan and peeled the first layer of your onion, read through this workbook again. It and all you have written in it will help you when you are ready to start peeling the next layer.

Personal onion-peeling is a process that needs to be carefully worked through, just as you would in any well-run business. This workbook will help you do that in a very thorough, effective way, so that ultimately you can proceed with confidence, peeling through layer upon layer as you work toward your life goals. So, good luck! And, let's start peeling onions!

SESSION 1

INTRODUCTION TO ONION PEELING

Session 1
Introduction

INTRODUCTION TO ONION PEELING

This session introduces you to the onion peeling process. You will be hearing a little more about how I developed the process, including two discoveries I made along the way that make this process unique.

Then you will explore just what this process can do for you personally. You will learn the primary goal and purposes of onion peeling and the benefits it offers. You next will examine the basic elements of the process and see how the natural planning steps involved are similar to the informal decision-making you do every day.

Also during this session, you will have the opportunity to get to know your workshop facilitator and fellow workshop participants. With them, you will be sharing your reasons for joining this life growth group and what you hope to get out of it.

Session 1
Goals

GOALS OF SESSION 1

The goals of this introductory session are to help you:

1. Overview the onion peeling process: how it was developed, its goal, purposes and benefits to you.

2. Understand the basic elements of the onion peeling process.

3. Understand the similarities between the natural planning process and your own informal decision-making process.

4. Get to know your fellow workshop participants and why they joined this life-growth group.

5. Join with workshop participants in an informal verbal contract to participate in the onion peeling life growth group.

Session 1
Workshop Activities

1. Facilitator's Introduction

    During this introduction, your facilitator will tell you how he or she learned to use the onion peeling process. You may wish to make a note of any information about onion peeling that may be useful to you.

    Notes:

2. Lecture Overviewing the Onion Peeling Process

    In this activity, you will learn how the onion peeling process was developed and what are its basic elements and benefits to you.

    Notes:

Session 1
Workshop Activities

3. Exercise: Exploring My Own Onion-Peeling Process

   Directions: Please write your answers to the following questions.

   1. A personal problem I recently worked on was:

   2. This problem was 1) Directly, 2) Indirectly, 3) not at all (circle one) related to my goal(s) in life.

   3. This problem was connected to one of my (1) most important (2) average, (3) least important (circle one) personal needs.

   4. The plan I followed to resolve this problem was:

   5. Times when I reviewed my progress in accomplishing this plan were:

   6. Adjustments (if any) I had to make in my plans were:

Session 1
Workshop Activities

4. Facilitator Review of the Exercise

   During this review, your facilitator will point out the similarity of your personal planning process to the onion process.

   Notes:

5. Why I Joined This Life-Growth Group

   Directions: With another workshop participant, please do the following:

   1. Introduce yourself.

   2. Describe what point you feel you are at in your life.

   3. Share your answers to these questions:

      a. A really positive experience I recently had was_____.

      b. One of the biggest challenges I face today is _____.

      c. My goal in life is to _____.

      d. On a scale of 1 to 10, with 10 the highest, I feel today about number ____ in comfort, and number _____ in willingness to take a risk.

      e. The most important reason for my joining this life-growth group is_____.

Session 1
Workshop Activities

6. What I Agreed To in the Workshop Contract

   Your workshop facilitator will be asking you to agree to an informal contract concerning the extent of your participation in this workshop. Please write what you agreed to in the space below.

   Notes:

7. Lecture on the Seven Rules of Planning

   In this activity, you will learn some basic rules for effective planning.

   Notes:

Session 1
Workshop Activities

8 Exercise: What The Seven Rules of Planning Mean to Me.

Directions: Below are the seven rules of planning. Please write an illustration of an individual (preferably yourself) using each rule. Rule No. 1 is already filled in as an example.

Rule 1: Each individual must do his or her planning.
Example: I decided on a new career and developed a two-year plan to prepare for it.

Rule 2: You must have an intimate knowledge of yourself.

Rule 3: You must be open to accepting the risk of change.

Rule 4: You must be free from pressure for immediate results from your plan.

Rule 5: Planning must be ongoing and continuous.

Rule 6: Precise analysis and creative imagination must be used.

Rule 7: Planning must always result in action.

Session 1
Workshop Activities

9. Session Summary

   This summary is a review of the onion peeling process and the seven rules of planning.

   Notes:

Session 1
Reading Assignments

SESSION 1: READING ASSIGNMENT

Please read the following chapters in the book, <u>Peel Your Own Onion</u>.

<u>CHAPTER 1: Goals</u>

    Notes:

<u>CHAPTER 2: The "Aha!" Chart</u>

    Notes:

Session 1
Journal Assignment

SESSION 1: JOURNAL ASSIGNMENT

Directions: Please write your answers to the following questions before the next session.

1. My goal in life is to:

2. I am or am not taking responsibility for my life. (Explain)

3. Names of self-profit people I know are:

4. I think the characteristics of "self-profit" people are:

5. Roadblocks I have set up in my road to self-profit are:

6. False goals I am pursuing are:

7. I hope the onion-peeling process can help me eliminate my roadblocks and false goals by:

Session 1
Journal Assignment

8. The point I was at after my last life-growth session was:

9. Insights I gained today related to my onion-peeling process are:

10. Things I talked to others today related to my onion-peeling process are:

11. Today, I'm at this point:

12. I'm ready to try these things:

13. Thoughts on my progress toward self-profit are:

MY EVALUATION OF SESSION 1

Please help us to evaluate the effectiveness of the workshop session in which you just participated by answering the following questions. Then give your completed questionnaire to your workshop facilitator at the next session.

1. Of how much value to you were the activities in this session?

    ____ a. Much value

    ____ b. Some value

    ____ c. Little value

    ____ d. No value

2. Did you increase your self-understanding during this session?

    ____ a. Yes

    ____ b. No

    ____ c. Uncertain

3. Did your confidence in resolving your problems increase as a result of this session?

    ____ a. Yes

    ____ b. No

    ____ c. Uncertain

4. Which activity or activities did you like the most? (You need only write the activity numbers given in the workbook.)

    _____

5. Which activity or activities did you like the least? (Again, just write their activity numbers here.)

    _____

6. Of the activity or activities you liked the least, what would you recommend we do to improve them?

    _____

    _____

    _____

    _____

(Please continue on to the next Page)

7. Was the amount of time spent in discussion during this session satisfactory?

   ____ a. Yes

   ____ b. No, too much time spent in discussion

   ____ c. No, too little time spent in discussion

8. Were there any additional activities you would have liked to participate in during this session? If so, what might they be?

   _____
   _____
   _____
   _____
   _____

Thank you for helping us out! Please remember to give this questionnaire to your workshop facilitator at the next session.

SESSION 2

STARTING WITH THE AHA! CHART

Session 2
Introduction

STARTING WITH THE AHA! CHART

Like any well run business, your own personal enterprise, I, Inc., needs a solid understanding of your basic functions or needs. Only then can you accurately identify which of your needs currently are not being met and undergo a plan of action to resolve the problems that result from them.

In this session, you'll learn about a function or needs chart I've developed to help you readily identify your unmet needs. I call it the Aha! Chart because very often people exclaim "Aha!" when they look at this chart and pinpoint exactly what needs are not being met in their lives. Some are surprised to find that their real problems lie in need areas they've overlooked while they have been pursuing other needs!

You'll be spending some time in this and the next session examining the Aha! Chart because needs frequently are difficult to identify and separate from one another. At the end of this session, however, you'll have a good idea of what your basic needs are. You'll also know how the Aha! Chart is used in the onion-peeling process. NOTE: For your convenience, an "Aha! Chart poster is included in your kit. You may wish to hang up this poster at home to help you continuously survey your needs.

Session 2
Goals

GOALS OF SESSION 2

The goals of this session are to help you:

1. Understand the purposes of the Aha! Chart.

2. Understand the following basic needs listed in the Aha! Chart:

   a. Physiological needs

   b. Safety needs

   c. Love needs

   d. Self-esteem needs

3. Learn how the Aha! Chart is used in the onion-peeling process.

Session 2
Workshop Activities

1. Journal Report

   During this group activity, you will be discussing your journal entries and any new insights you gained since the last workshop session.

   Notes:

2. Case Study Lecture

   This lecture presents a case study of an individual with a number of unmet needs and related problems. Listen carefully and see if you can identify what needs are not being met.

   Notes:

Session 2
Workshop Activities

3 Exercise: Case Study Review

Directions: In your own words, please describe five problems faced by the individual in the case study you just heard.

Problem No. 1:

Problem No. 2:

Problem No. 3:

Problem No. 4:

Problem No. 5:

Session 2
Workshop Activities

4. Facilitator Review of the Exercise

   In this activity, your facilitator will discuss with you the problems of the individual in the case study. You may wish to make a note of any new insights you gained about identifying unmet needs and their related problems.

   Notes:

5. Lecture on the "Aha!" Chart

   This lecture will introduce you to a chart you can use to identify your unmet needs.

   Notes:

Session 2
Workshop Activities

6. Small Group Discussion of a Case Study

Directions: Below is a case study of an individual with a number of unmet needs and related problems. Read it over and then answer the questions below. Be prepared to share your answers and the reasons for them with the entire workshop group after you finish this discussion.

Allen, a twenty-eight year old research scientist, accepted an exciting job offer that required him to leave his home town and move to California. The decision to take the job was a hard one. Allen was very close to his parents and was reluctant to leave them, particularly because his father was ailing at the time. He also had a number of good friends in his home town, and he worried about getting out of touch with them. Although he joked with others about "my anxiety over leaving the nest," he was deeply concerned about how he could maintain these relationships when he moved to California.

Once he made the move, he found his job every bit as exciting and challenging as he had anticipated it would be. One problem that became immediately apparent, however, was the long hours of work the job required. He spent many nights and weekends at the research laboratory where he worked, and he wondered when he would get some free time, especially vacation time, to go home and see his parents and friends. By looking at his upcoming work schedule, he could see he might not even be able to fly home for Christmas, a time when his relatives traditionally met for their "family reunion."

While he liked living in California, he hadn't much time to meet new friends other than those he gained through his work at the laboratory. Being single, he missed the social life and dating he enjoyed at home. He wondered just how he was going to find the time and opportunities he needed to develop new relationships.

1. Where are the needs of this person located on the Aha! Chart?

2. Which needs are not being met now?

3. Which needs appear to be in conflict?

Session 2
Workshop Activities

7. Small Group Discussion on Meanings of Aha! Chart Needs

   Directions: (1) Discuss with your group any questions you have about the boxes in the Aha! Chart. (2) Then share three personal examples of needs you have and point out where they appear on the chart. Be prepared to share these examples with the entire workshop group in the next activity.

8. Large Group Discussion of the Aha! Chart

   During this discussion, you will continue your examination of the Aha! Chart. You also will share with the group some examples of your own needs. You may wish to make a note of any new insights you have gained during this discussion concerning your needs.

   Notes:

Session 2
Workshop Activities

9   Session Summary

This summary is a review of the Aha! Chart and its boxes.

Notes:

Session 2
Reading Assignment

SESSION 2: READING ASSIGNMENT

Review Chapter 2 in the book, Peel Your Own Onion, and make notes on new insights you have gained since your first reading.

CHAPTER 2: The "Aha!" Chart

    Notes:

Session 2
Journal Assignment

SESSION 2: JOURNAL ASSIGNMENT - PART 1

Directions: Please write your answers to the following questions before the next session.

1. Thoughts I have about my unfulfilled needs are:

2. Thoughts on how my unfulfilled needs affect my life are:

3. Names of my significant friends are:

4. The role of my significant friends in my life is:

5. The point I was at after my last life-growth group session was:

6. Insights I gained today related to my onion-peeling process are:

7. Things I talked to others about today related to my onion-peeling process are:

Session 2
Journal Assignment

8. Today, I'm at this point:

9. I'm ready to try these things:

10. Thoughts on my progress toward self profit are:

Please continue on to the next page and complete Part 2 of the Journal Assignment.

Session 2
Journal Assignment

SESSION 2: JOURNAL ASSIGNMENT - PART 2

Directions: Please write your answers to the following questions. They will help you explore each need identified in the Aha! Chart as it pertains to you. Take as much time as you need - even days - to think over your answers.

1. In the past, I was best able to provide for my physiological needs when:_____
   _____.

2. I felt the healthiest when:_____
   _____.

3. I felt the least fear and the most security when:_____
   _____.

4. I felt the closest to the people I know when:_____
   _____.

5. Rituals have been the most important to me when:_____
   _____.

6. The time when I felt conformity was important were:___
   _____.

7. I was most creative when:_____
   _____.

8. The people I have given love the most to are:_____
   _____.

9. The people I received the most love from are:_____
   _____.

10. I was the most immature in my loving when:_____
    _____.

-30-

Session 2
Journal Assignment

11. I was the most mature in my loving when:_____
_____.

12. I feel I had the greatest self love when:_____
_____.

13. I satisfied my spiritual love needs by:_____
_____.

14. The friends I have loved and who loved me in return were:
_____
_____.

15. My love of my parents and their love for me was the strongest when:_____
_____.

16. I was best able to fulfill my erotic love needs when:_____
_____.

17. I felt others respected me most when:_____
_____.

18. I respected myself the most when:_____
_____.

19. I was most productive in my work when:_____
_____.

20. I felt the most pleasure when:_____
_____.

21. I felt the most confident when:_____
_____.

22. I usually had a respect for facts when:_____
_____.

Session 2
Journal Assignment

23. The times when I felt unearned guilt were: _____
_____

24. My mind was best able to influence my feelings when: _____
_____.

25. I had the greatest will to understand when: _____
_____.

MY EVALUATION OF SESSION 2

Please help us to evaluate the effectiveness of the workshop session in which you just participated by answering the following questions. Then give your completed questionnaire to your workshop facilitator at the next session.

1. Of how much value to you were the activities in this session?

    ____ a. Much value

    ____ b. Some value

    ____ c. Little value

    ____ d. No value

2. Did you increase your self-understanding during this session?

    ____ a. Yes

    ____ b. No

    ____ c. Uncertain

3. Did your confidence in resolving your problems increase as a result of this session?

    ____ a. Yes

    ____ b. No

    ____ c. Uncertain

4. Which activity or activities did you like the most? (You need only write the activity numbers given in the workbook.)

    _____

5. Which activity or activities did you like the least? (Again, just write their activity numbers here.)

    _____

6. Of the activity or activities you liked the least, what would you recommend we do to improve them?

    _____
    _____
    _____
    _____

(Please continue on to the next Page)

7. Was the amount of time spent in discussion during this session satisfactory?

   ____ a. Yes

   ____ b. No, too much time spent in discussion

   ____ c. No, too little time spent in discussion

8. Were there any additional activities you would have liked to participate in during this session? If so, what might they be?

   _____

   _____

   _____

   _____

   _____

Thank you for helping us out! Please remember to give this questionnaire to your workshop facilitator at the next session.

SESSION 3

IDENTIFYING YOUR NEEDS

Session 3
Introduction

IDENTIFYING YOUR NEEDS

In the last session, you examined the many needs all of us experience in life and you saw these needs laid out in the Aha! Chart. Now it's time to use the chart to identify your unmet needs and make a list of the problems you would like to resolve on the way to maximizing your self-profit.

The goal of this session is to help you identify at least five unmet needs in your life, so be prepared to do some careful thinking about them. In later sessions, you will pick the most important unmet need and its associated problem to work on for your first onion-peeling project.

Session 3
Goals

GOALS OF SESSION 3

The goals of this session are to help you:

1. Examine the state of your needs today and identify high and low need areas.

2. Use the Aha! Chart to identify at least five unmet needs in your life.

3. Write statements accurately describing these problems in order to more clearly understand them.

Session 3
Workshop Activities

1. Journal Report

   During this group activity, you will be discussing your journal entries and any new insights you gained since the last workshop session.

   Notes:

2. Case Study Lecture

   In this lecture, your workshop facilitator will use the Aha! Chart to show the fulfilled and unfulfilled needs of an individual in a case study. You may wish to make a note of any new information you have learned concerning the Aha! Chart and how to use it.

   Notes:

Session 3
Workshop Activities

3. Small Group Discussion of My Needs

   Directions: Review the answers you gave in Part 2 of the journal assignment for Session 2 (page 30). Then write your answers to the following questions and share your responses with your small group.

   1. The questions I learned the most from were: _____
   _____

   Explain.

   2. When writing my responses to these questions, I was surprised to discover that:

   3. Need areas I should think more about are:

Session 3
Workshop Activities

4 Exercise: The Status of My Needs Today.

Directions: Assess the present status of your needs by rating them on a scale of 1-10, with ten being the highest.

NEED	STATUS
1. Self-Profit	_____
2. Physiological Needs	_____
3. Safety Needs	_____
4. General Love Needs	_____
5. Rituals	_____
6. Conformity	_____
7. Creative Activity	_____
8. Giving and Receiving Love	_____
9. Immature Love	_____
10. Mature Love	_____
11. Self Love	_____
12. Spiritual Love	_____
13. Friend Love	_____
14. Parental Love	_____
15. Erotic Love	_____
16. General Esteem Needs	_____
17. Productive Work	_____
18. Pleasure	_____
19. Self-Respect/Self-Confidence	_____
20. Respect for Facts	_____
21. Unearned Guilt	_____
22. Mind Over Feelings	_____
23. Will to Understand	_____

Session 3
Workshop Activities

5. Large Group Discussion: My High and Low Need Areas

During this discussion, you will be sharing with the workshop group the high and low need areas you identified in the previous activity. You may wish to make a note of any points made that adds to your understanding of your needs.

Notes:

Session 3
Workshop Activities

6. Exercise: Pinpointing My Problems

Directions: Review the present status of your needs as you determined them in Activity 3.04 and try to identify possible unmet needs in your life. Make a list of these in the space provided below. Then write a description of the problem that results from each unmet need (Note: Write your problem statements in pencil. You may want to erase and rewrite them as you proceed through the workshop sessions.)

MY UNMET NEEDS   PROBLEM STATEMENTS

1._____   1._____
                                          _____
                                          _____

2._____   2._____
                                          _____
                                          _____

3._____   3._____
                                          _____
                                          _____

4._____   4._____
                                          _____
                                          _____

5._____   5._____
                                          _____
                                          _____

PLEASE CONTINUE ON TO THE NEXT PAGE.

Session 3
Workshop Activities

MY UNMET NEEDS   PROBLEM STATEMENTS

6._____   6._____
                                _____
                                _____

7._____   7._____
                                _____
                                _____
                                _____

8._____   8._____
                                _____
                                _____
                                _____

9._____   9._____
                                _____
                                _____

10._____   10._____
                                _____
                                _____

Session 3
Workshop Activities

7. Large Group Discussion: Problem Statements

   During this discussion, you will be sharing with the workshop groups the problem statements you wrote in the previous activity. Constructive criticism of these statements will help you to clarify your understanding of your problems.

   Notes:

8. Session Summary

   This summary reviews the Aha! Chart and the usefulness of writing problem statements.

   Notes:

Session 3
Reading Assignment

SESSION 3: READING ASSIGNMENT

Read the following chapters in the book, <u>Peel Your Own Onion</u>.

<u>CHAPTER 3: THE RULES OF PLANNING</u>

Notes:

<u>CHAPTER 4: SETTING YOUR PRIORITIES</u>

Notes:

Session 3
Journal Assignments

SESSION 3: JOURNAL ASSIGNMENTS

Directions: Please write your answers to the following questions.

1. Which of the seven rules of planning will be the hardest for you to learn to use? Why?

2. The point I was at after my last life-growth session was:

3. Insights I gained today related to my onion-peeling process are:

4. Things I talked to others about today related to my onion-peeling process are:

5. Today, I'm at this point:

6. I'm ready to try these things:

7. Thoughts on my progress toward self-profit are:

MY EVALUATION OF SESSION 3

Please help us to evaluate the effectiveness of the workshop session in which you just participated by answering the following questions. Then give your completed questionnaire to your workshop facilitator at the next session.

1. Of how much value to you were the activities in this session?

    ____ a. Much value

    ____ b. Some value

    ____ c. Little value

    ____ d. No value

2. Did you increase your self-understanding during this session?

    ____ a. Yes

    ____ b. No

    ____ c. Uncertain

3. Did your confidence in resolving your problems increase as a result of this session?

    ____ a. Yes

    ____ b. No

    ____ c. Uncertain

4. Which activity or activities did you like the most? (You need only write the activity numbers given in the workbook.)

    _____

5. Which activity or activities did you like the least? (Again, just write their activity numbers here.)

    _____

6. Of the activity or activities you liked the least, what would you recommend we do to improve them?

    _____
    _____
    _____
    _____

(Please continue on to the next Page)

7. Was the amount of time spent in discussion during this session satisfactory?

   ____ a. Yes

   ____ b. No, too much time spent in discussion

   ____ c. No, too little time spent in discussion

8. Were there any additional activities you would have liked to participate in during this session? If so, what might they be?

   _____
   _____
   _____
   _____
   _____

Thank you for helping us out! Please remember to give this questionnaire to your workshop facilitator at the next session.

SESSION 4

PRIORITY SETTING

Session 4
Introduction

PRIORITY SETTING

In this session, you will learn which of your problems are really the most important to you by giving them priorities. Your top priority problem will be the first one you will plan to resolve through the onion-peeling process.

Too often we try to deal simultaneously with a number of problems in our lives with the result that some problems are neglected while plans for others fall by the wayside. Very often the problem in which we are investing a good portion of our energies turns out to be not the problem that is the most important to us! The "pairing method" I introduce in this session will help you to see your problems in the real order of their importance to you.

During the first activities in this session, you will review the seven rules of planning. Then you will use priority setting to evaluate the importance to you of each of the problem statements you developed during the last session. Once you have accomplished this important step in the onion peeling process, you will be ready to create a plan of action to resolve your top priority problem.

Session 4
Goals

GOALS OF SESSION 4

The goals of this session are to help you:

1. Use the seven rules of planning in your onion peeling process.

2. Learn the technique of priority setting.

3. Use priority setting to identify the most important problem in your life at this time.

Session 4
Workshop Activities

1. Journal Report

    During this group activity, you will discuss your journal entries and any new insights you gained since the last workshop session.

    Notes:

2. Lecture on the Seven Rules of Planning

    This lecture reviews the seven rules of planning and their importance in onion peeling.

    Notes:

Session 4
Workshop Activities

3. Small Group Activity on the Seven Rules of Planning

Directions: Below are the seven rules of planning and descriptions of people implementing or trying to implement them. Discuss each example with your group. Then place a "C" before the example if it illustrates conforming to the rule or a "V" if it illustrates a violation of the rule.

Rule No. 1.   Each individual must do his or her own planning.

_____   Example: A salesman returns to college to prepare for a career as a lawyer because "that is the one vocation my father feels is the most worth pursuing."

_____   Example: A woman asks her husband to critique her plans for starting a small business.

Rule No. 2.   You must have an intimate knowledge of yourself.

_____   Example: A woman goes into therapy sessions with a psychologist to learn more about herself.

_____   Example: A businessman asks his associate to "share your observations on how I behave with our clients."

Rule No. 3.   You must be open to accepting the risk of change.

_____   Example: A man remains in an unrewarding job "because I know my position here is secure."

_____   Example: A woman drops out of Alcoholics Anonymous "because I'll lose the companionship of all my drinking friends."

Rule No. 4.   You must be free from pressure for immediate results from your plan.

_____   Example: A woman saves money for four months living expenses so she can quit her job and study to become a stockbroker.

_____   Example: A salesman plans to double his income "within the next year or get out of this business."

PLEASE CONTINUE ON TO NEXT PAGE.

Session 4
Workshop Activities

Rule No. 5.   Planning must be ongoing and continuous.

_____   Example: A man puts his retirement savings in a separate bank "so I can just forget about it and let the interest grow."

_____   Example: A married couple changes their children's college trust fund when they learn of a more effective trust plan offered by their bank.

Rule No. 6.   Precise analysis and creative imagination must be used.

_____   Example: When planning to build his own lake cabin, a man creates an alternative plan for hiring a building contractor "if later on I find this project to be just too much work."

_____   Example: Two widows discuss new ways to meet friends and increase their social lives.

Rule No. 7.   Planning must always result in action.

_____   Example: A man plans to write a novel someday.

_____   Example: Two woman plan to quit smoking next week and to monitor each other's progress.

Session 4
Workshop Activities

4. Exercise: What Would Happen If....?

   Directions: With another workshop participant, discuss your answers to the following questions.

   1. What would happen if you wanted to begin a new career and you made your parent(s), spouse, or friend a co-planner?

   2. What would happen if you set a deadline of 30 days for resolving a relationship problem with someone close to you?

   3. What would happen if you invested all your money in a small business you felt could run by itself without your supervision?

Session 4
Workshop Activities

5. Follow Up to the Exercise

   This activity is a large group discussion of the questions you just considered. You may wish to make a note of any points made that increases your understanding of the seven rules of planning.

   Notes:

6. Lecture on Priority Setting

   This lecture uses a case study to illustrate the "pairing method" used in priority setting.

   Notes:

-50-

Session 4
Workshop Activities

7. Exercise: Priority Setting

Directions: Read over the following case study of how one individual performed priority setting. Then answer the questions on the following page.

Note: This is a continuation of a case study you considered in Activity 2.06.

Three months after Allen arrived in California for his new job, he sat down to consider the problems he was facing at that time. He spent a week reflecting on his unmet needs and writing problem statements that accurately defined those needs and the challenges they represented. Then he had a friend from work critique the statements, which helped him to clarify his understanding of his problems.

He then set aside a Saturday afternoon for "a little priority setting." He decided to use the pairing method he had learned in the Peel Your Own Onion Workshop. He made a list of his problem statements and compared them one to another in a series of rounds. After comparing problem #1 with all his other problems and giving a score of one to the problem that seemed most important to him, he went on to compare problem #2 with the others, and so on. He started out being "rather analytical" about each problem, but soon decided it was better to trust his feelings in determining which problems were more important to him than others.

Initially, he felt that his problem was "my parental needs are suffering as a result of my new job making me inaccessible to my parents" would be his top priority problem. He was interested to find out if this would be true after he had set his priorities using the pairing method.

Here is his completed list of prioritized problems:

PLEASE CONTINUE ON TO THE NEXT PAGE.

-51-

PROBLEM STATEMENTS	ROUND 1	ROUND 2	ROUND 3	ROUND 4	TOTALS
1. My parental love needs suffer as a result of my new job making me unaccessible to my parents.	111				3
2. My friend love needs are neglected because my job makes me unaccessible to old friends back in my home town.		1			1
3. My friend love needs are neglected because my busy job leaves me little time to meet new friends here in California.		1	1		2
4. My erotic love needs suffer as a result of my having little time to pursue social relationships.	1	1	1	1	4
5. My pleasure needs suffer as a result of my having little off-work time to pursue hobbies and other creative activities.					0

PLEASE CONTINUE ON TO THE NEXT PAGE.

Session 4
Workshop Activities

1. What were the priority setting steps the individual in the example followed?

2. What is this person's top priority problem?

3. Was this top priority problem the one he originally thought to be the most important to him?

Session 4
Workshop Activities

8. Prioritizing My Problem Statements
   Directions: Write in abbreviated form the problem statements you developed during the last session in the space provided. Then prioritize them using the pairing method. NOTE: If you have more than ten problem statements, use a separate piece of paper.

PROBLEM STATEMENTS	ROUND 1	ROUND 2	ROUND 3	ROUND 4	ROUND 5	ROUND 6	ROUND 7	ROUND 8	ROUND 9	TOTALS
1.										
2.										
3.										
4.										
5.										
6.										
7.										
8.										
9.										
10.										

Session 4
Workshop Activities

9. Session Summary

This summary is a review of the seven rules of planning and the "pairing method" used in priority setting.

Notes:

Session 4
Reading Assignment

SESSION 4: READING ASSIGNMENT

Read the following chapters in the book, <u>Peel Your Own Onion</u>.

<u>CHAPTER 5: THE PLANNING SEQUENCE</u>

Notes:

<u>CHAPTER 6: THE ENVIRONMENT</u>

Notes:

Session 4
Journal Assignment

SESSION 4: JOURNAL ASSIGNMENT

Directions: Please write your answers to the following questions before the next session.

1. Please record your thoughts and feelings on how each of the seven rules of planning will impact your life. (For example, you may have decided to be more assertive in doing your own planning. Therefore, your response to Rule No. 1 might be: "I will not ask anyone to critique my plans until I have them well thought out and written down."

    Rule No. 1   Each individual must do his or her own planning.

    Rule No. 2   You must have an intimate knowledge of yourself.

    Rule No. 3   You must be open to accepting the risk of change.

    Rule No. 4   You must be free from pressure for immediate results from your plan.

    Rule No. 5   Planning must be ongoing and continuous.

    Rule No. 6   Precise analysis and creative imagination must be used.

    Rule No. 7   Planning must always result in action.

Session 4
Journal Assignment

2. Are any of your high priorities based on your desire to change other people? If so, do you think you may become frustrated and unsuccessful?

3. Do you feel you have matched your priorities with needs you are trying to change? (For example, are you trying to overcome a deficiency in your love needs by working on your esteem needs?)

4. The point I was at after my last life-growth session was:

5. Insights I gained today related to my onion-peeling process are:

6. Things I talked to others about today related to my onion-peeling process are:

7. Today I'm at this point:

8. I'm ready to try these things:

9. Thoughts on my progress toward self-profit are:

MY EVALUATION OF SESSION 4

Please help us to evaluate the effectiveness of the workshop session in which you just participated by answering the following questions. Then give your completed questionnaire to your workshop facilitator at the next session.

1. Of how much value to you were the activities in this session?

    ____ a. Much value

    ____ b. Some value

    ____ c. Little value

    ____ d. No value

2. Did you increase your self-understanding during this session?

    ____ a. Yes

    ____ b. No

    ____ c. Uncertain

3. Did your confidence in resolving your problems increase as a result of this session?

    ____ a. Yes

    ____ b. No

    ____ c. Uncertain

4. Which activity or activities did you like the most? (You need only write the activity numbers given in the workbook.)

    _____

5. Which activity or activities did you like the least? (Again, just write their activity numbers here.)

    _____

6. Of the activity or activities you liked the least, what would you recommend we do to improve them?

    _____
    _____
    _____
    _____

(Please continue on to the next Page)

7. Was the amount of time spent in discussion during this session satisfactory?

   ____ a. Yes

   ____ b. No, too much time spent in discussion

   ____ c. No, too little time spent in discussion

8. Were there any additional activities you would have liked to participate in during this session? If so, what might they be?

   _____

   _____

   _____

   _____

   _____

Thank you for helping us out! Please remember to give this questionnaire to your workshop facilitator at the next session.

SESSION 5

INTRODUCTION TO THE PLANNING PROCESS

Session 5
Introduction

INTRODUCTION TO THE PLANNING PROCESS

As I stated in my book, one of my major discoveries is that all of us have a natural planning process we use in routinely solving problems. Psychologists point out that we do much of this planning subconsciously with a "trial and error" approach to dealing with our problems. For minor problems, this approach may be acceptable. Yet when we are confronted with more complex problems, the "trial and error" method proves to be as haphazard and inefficient as throwing a basketball blindly over one's shoulders with the hope that the hoop will somehow be in its path of descent and you'll win the game!

Chapter 5 in my book introduced you to a more systematic way of planning to resolve your problems. In this session, you'll explore this planning process in more depth. Specifically, you'll be examining the environmental factors that play so important a role in planning: What these factors are and why they must be taken into consideration. In the next session, you will then work on identifying the environmental factors that relate to the specific problem you have decided to "peel" during this workshop.

Session 5
Goals

GOALS OF SESSION 5

The goals of this session are to help you:

1. Explore the benefits to you of using the natural planning sequence.

2. Become thoroughly familiar with the four environmental factors considered in the natural planning sequence:

   a. Internal factors
   b. External factors
   c. Expectations
   d. Stakeholder needs

Session 5
Workshop Activities

1. Journal Report

   During this group activity, you will discuss your journal entries and any new insights you have gained since the last workshop session.

   Notes:

2. Lecture on The Natural Planning Sequence

   This lecture overviews the natural planning sequence. It also points out the difference between "muddy water planning" and natural planning.

   Notes:

Session 5
Workshop Activities

3. Exercise: Identifying Environmental Factors

   Directions: In front of each example, place the letter of the environmental factor to which it belongs. The examples refer to a person whose problem statement is:

   "I am dissatisfied with my present job which is causing me loss of self-esteem and self-profit because of the job's lack of creative opportunities."

   EXAMPLE

   ____ 1. Chances for being promoted into a more rewarding job position are nil.

   ____ 2. I haven't explored new job opportunities

   ____ 3. I need greater self-esteem and self-profit, especially through my work.

   ____ 4. I hope to find a satisfying new source of productive work within the next two years.

   ____ 5. I don't fully understand what sort of creative opportunities I would like in a job.

   ____ 6. Financial obligations prevent me from going back to school to prepare for a new career.

   ____ 7. My spouse needs my continued financial support, but also an improved relationship with me that would result if I were happier in my work.

   ____ 8. The need to fulfill my family obligations may limit some of my options, but ultimately, I will succeed.

   ____ 9. My children need my companionship and guidance; no sacrifices while I pursue a solution to this problem.

   ENVIRONMENTAL FACTORS

   A. Internal factors
   B. External factors
   C. Expectations
   D. Stakeholder needs

Session 5
Workshop Activities

_____ 10. I hope to discover just what type of creative work will maximize my self-profit, but I realize this won't happen overnight.

Session 5
Workshop Activities

4. Small Group Analysis of a Case Study

Directions: Below is a case study of an individual undergoing the natural planning sequence. Read it over and answer the questions on the following page. Then share your answers with the group.

THE PROBLEM

Mary, a divorced woman with two young children, looked at the Aha! Chart and identified a number of unmet needs and related problems she currently was facing. When she prioritized these problems using the pairing method, she discovered her top priority problem involved not only her, but also her children. Her problem statement for this was: "My spiritual needs and those of my children are not being met as a result of our not being involved in any organized religious activities." The problem involved not only selecting a church, but also a denomination.

THE ENVIRONMENTAL FACTORS

Her first thought was to identify some of the internal factors she would change in her life and the lives of her children in order to resolve the problem. She hadn't spent much time thinking about her religious beliefs lately, nor had she talked much with her children about religion. Neither had she entered her children in any church school program. While she was brought up as a Congregationalist, she had never really compared this denomination with others to see what they might offer her and her children. These were all things she knew she could and should do.

When she thought about it, Mary realized there were very few external factors she could not change with respect to this problem. She had no family pressure to remain a Congregationalist, nor did she have any strong biases against any other denomination. The only thing she felt firmly about was that any church she and her children attended had to be near her home or at least in the surburb in which she lived.

PLEASE CONTINUE ON TO THE NEXT PAGE.

Session 5
Workshop Activities

Since she felt exploring and confirming one's religious beliefs is a life long venture, Mary did not expect that she and her children would undergo "a genuine religious conversion" or commitment to a denomination soon. But she did feel it was realistic to expect to find a source of religious education for her children this year, plus a church community she could join while she was exploring her own religious beliefes.

She knew she needed to fill this "spiritual gap" in her life and to confirm and express her spiritual love through organized church activities. She also had a need for community with others, a need she felt a church could help to fulfill. Her children needed to develop their own capacities for spiritual love and to learn the meaning of religion and its role in their lives. She also knew her parents were very concerned about her children's spiritual welfare. These were the major stakeholder needs she knew she had to take into consideration when she would start to plan to resolve the problem:

Directions: Next to each step in the Action Plan below, write which environmental factors it seems to take into consideration: external factors, internal factors, expectations, or stakeholder needs. Then share your answers with the group and discuss which environmental factors were involved in each step.

THE ACTION PLAN

Mary's Action Plan was as follows

Environmental Factors
Considered   My Strategic Plan

_____   My children and I currently have no organized way of meeting our spiritual needs. I want to involve us in educational and worship activities in a church as soon as possible.

                   My Management Plan

_____   1. Go to library; research and compare the different denominations.

_____   2. Make a list of the religious beliefs I have now.

_____   3. Start discussing religion with my children.

_____   4. Make a list of local churches; contact them and ask for information about each.

_____   5. Visit these churches.

_____   6. Select a church and enroll children in its church school program.

Session 5
Workshop Activities

_____ 7. Discuss with children what they learned at church school.

_____ 8. Get personally involved in at least one organized function of the church.

_____ 9. Attend church regularly.

_____ 10. Show this plan to my parents; ask for their help.

<u>My Operational Plan</u>

_____ 1. Read about and compare the different denominations this year.

_____ 2. Make a list of my religious beliefs and complete it this week.

_____ 3. Begin discussing religion with my children this week.

_____ 4. Contact local churches this week.

_____ 5. Visit one new church a week for the next two months.

_____ 6. By May 1st, select a church and enroll my children in its church school program.

_____ 7. Each Sunday afternoon, discuss with my children what they learned that day at church school.

_____ 8. By June 1st, get involved in at least one organized church activity other than the worship services.

_____ 9. Start attending church regularly now.

_____ 10. Show this plan to my parents this week.

Session 5
Workshop Activities

5. Clarifying My Problem Statement

    Directions: Reconsider your top priority problem statement. Are there any changes you would like to make in the statement, considering what you have learned about environmental factors? If so, what are they? Write the new draft of your problem statement below.

My Top Priority Problem:_____

_____

_____

_____

_____

6. Session Summary

    This summary is a review of the natural planning sequence.

    Notes:

SESSION 5: READING ASSIGNMENT

Read the following chapter in the book, Peel Your Own Onion.

CHAPTER 7: THE PLANS

Notes:

Session 5
Journal Assignment

SESSION 5: JOURNAL ASSIGNMENT

Directions: Please write your answers to the following questions.

1. The benefits to me from using the natural planning process are:

2. The point I was at after my last life-growth session was:

3. Insights I gained today related to my onion-peeling process are:

4. Things I talked to others about today related to my onion-peeling process are:

5. Today, I'm at this point:

6. I'm ready to try these things:

7. Thoughts on my progress toward self-profit are:

MY EVALUATION OF SESSION 5

Please help us to evaluate the effectiveness of the workshop session in which you just participated by answering the following questions. Then give your completed questionnaire to your workshop facilitator at the next session.

1. Of how much value to you were the activities in this session?

    ____ a. Much value

    ____ b. Some value

    ____ c. Little value

    ____ d. No value

2. Did you increase your self-understanding during this session?

    ____ a. Yes

    ____ b. No

    ____ c. Uncertain

3. Did your confidence in resolving your problems increase as a result of this session?

    ____ a. Yes

    ____ b. No

    ____ c. Uncertain

4. Which activity or activities did you like the most? (You need only write the activity numbers given in the workbook.)
   _____

5. Which activity or activities did you like the least? (Again, just write their activity numbers here.)
   _____

6. Of the activity or activities you liked the least, what would you recommend we do to improve them?
   _____
   _____
   _____
   _____

(Please continue on to the next Page)

7. Was the amount of time spent in discussion during this session satisfactory?

　　____ a. Yes

　　____ b. No, too much time spent in discussion

　　____ c. No, too little time spent in discussion

8. Were there any additional activities you would have liked to participate in during this session? If so, what might they be?

_____

_____

_____

_____

_____

Thank you for helping us out! Please remember to give this questionnaire to your workshop facilitator at the next session.

SESSION 6

TAKING YOUR ENVIRONMENT INTO ACCOUNT

Session 6
Introduction

TAKING YOUR ENVIRONMENT INTO ACCOUNT

Taking your environment into account during the planning process is much like taking a picture with a camera. When you first snap the shutter button you "see" one picture. But very often when you get the film processed and have the printed photo in hand, you notice a lot more things going on in the photographed scene than you originally perceived! Similarly, during the planning process, your first thought of your environment gives you an overall but somewhat vague idea of the picture. But when you invest some time and careful thought in listing all the environmental factors involved, you have a far more complete picture to take into account when you start devising your action plan.

In this session, you will identify all the environmental factors that relate to the problem you have selected for your first onion-peeling project. By writing these factors down, you will get a much better "picture" of your problem, the environmental factors involved, and how much of a solution you think you can achieve.

Session 6
Goals

GOALS OF SESSION 6

The goals of this session are to help you:

1. Identify the environmental factors pertaining to your current top priority problem.

2. Evaluate your problem in light of the environmental factors involved.

Session 6
Workshop Activities

1. Journal Report

    During this group activity, you will discuss your journal entries and any new insights you have gained since the last workshop session.

    Notes:

2. Lecture Reviewing Environmental Factors

    This lecture provides you with helpful information on how to identify the environmental factors pertaining to your top priority problem.

    Notes:

Session 6
Workshop Activities

3. Exercise: Identifying My Environmental Factors

Directions: Write your problem statement in the space provided. Then list all the environmental factors you can think of that pertain to the problem. (Space is provided on this and the following page.) NOTE: Use a pencil in case you want to erase and write in new information later on.

My Top Priority Problem: _____

_____
_____
_____

INTERNAL FACTORS	EXTERNAL FACTORS

Session 6
Workshop Activities

EXPECTATIONS	STAKEHOLDER NEEDS

Session 6
Workshop Activities

4. Clarifying My Problem Statement and Environmental Factors

   Directions: Exchange your lists of environmental factors with another workshop participant. Use the following questions to help you analyze the other participant's list. Then discuss your lists with the participant and determine if you wish to make any clarifications or other changes in either your problem statement or your list of environmental factors.

INTERNAL FACTORS

1. Are these factors that can be changed?

2. Do they explore a variety of options?

EXTERNAL FACTORS

1. Are these factors that cannot be changed?

2. Do they pertain to the problem described?

EXPECTATIONS

1. Do these expectations express a realistic chance of achieving the objective stated?

2. Do these expectations indicate a positive commitment to pursuing the objective?

3. Do these expectations indicate factors that might limit the achievement of the objective?

STAKEHOLDERS NEEDS

1. Do you think all of the participant's major stakeholders have been listed?

2. Have the specific needs of the stakeholders been mentioned (especially those needs that might be affected by the problem or its solution)?

Session 6
Workshop Activities

5. Large Group Discussion on Environmental Factors

   In this discussion, you will be sharing your thoughts about your environmental factors and how they will affect your planning. You may wish to make a note of any points made that add to your understanding of your environmental factors.

   Notes:

6. Session Summary

   This summary reviews the role of environmental factors in the natural planning process.

   Notes:

Session 6
Reading Assignment

SESSION 6: READING ASSIGNMENT

Please read the following chapters in the book, <u>Peel Your Own Onion</u>.

CHAPTER 7: THE PLANS

Review this chapter and make notes on any new insights you have gained since your first reading.

Notes:

CHAPTER 8: ANALYSIS

Notes:

Session 6
Journal Assignment

SESSION 6: JOURNAL ASSIGNMENT

Directions: Please write your answers to the following questions.

1. I have or have not (circle one) expressed a positive expectation for achieving my plan. (Explain)

2. I think it is vital to express a positive expectation because:

3. The point I was at after my last life-growth session was:

4. Insights I gained today related to my onion-peeling process are:

5. Things I talked to others about today related to my onion-peeling process are:

6. Today, I'm at this point:

7. I'm ready to try these things:

8. Thoughts on my progress toward self-profit are:

Session 7
Introduction

YOUR ACTION PLAN

In Chapter 7 of my book, you read about a three-step plan for resolving problems: The Strategic Plan in which you identify your objective; the Management Plan in which you list actions that can be taken to achieve your objective; and the Operational Plan in which you develop a timetable for carrying out the actions. This is the planning process I have helped numerous business organizations adopt to effectively resolve financial, sales and management problems. Now I want to help you apply this process to your own personal business, I, Inc.

In this session, you first will review your problem statements and make any necessary changes in your lists of environmental factors affecting your problem. This process of review is a vital one! Everyday we learn more about ourselves and our environment. And this can only add to our understanding of our problems and how to resolve them!

Next you will explore the three-step planning process and how it can be carried out most effectively. Finally, you will create your own action plan for resolving your current top priority problem. (NOTE: For your convenience, a "Planning Sequence Chart" has been included in your workshop kit. You may wish to hang the chart on a wall in your home as a reminder of the steps that must be taken for successful onion peeling.)

I think you will find this the most productive session of the entire workshop. As hundreds of other former workshop participants (now accomplished onion-peelers!) have discovered, the investment of your time, careful thinking and creative imagination will result in a detailed plan of action - a major step forward in successfully resolving your problem!

MY EVALUATION OF SESSION 6

Please help us to evaluate the effectiveness of the workshop session in which you just participated by answering the following questions. Then give your completed questionnaire to your workshop facilitator at the next session.

1. Of how much value to you were the activities in this session?

    _____ a. Much value

    _____ b. Some value

    _____ c. Little value

    _____ d. No value

2. Did you increase your self-understanding during this session?

    _____ a. Yes

    _____ b. No

    _____ c. Uncertain

3. Did your confidence in resolving your problems increase as a result of this session?

    _____ a. Yes

    _____ b. No

    _____ c. Uncertain

4. Which activity or activities did you like the most? (You need only write the activity numbers given in the workbook.)

    _____

5. Which activity or activities did you like the least? (Again, just write their activity numbers here.)

    _____

6. Of the activity or activities you liked the least, what would you recommend we do to improve them?

    _____

    _____

    _____

    _____

(Please continue on to the next Page)

7. Was the amount of time spent in discussion during this session satisfactory?

   ____ a. Yes

   ____ b. No, too much time spent in discussion

   ____ c. No, too little time spent in discussion

8. Were there any additional activities you would have liked to participate in during this session? If so, what might they be?

   _____

   _____

   _____

   _____

   _____

Thank you for helping us out! Please remember to give this questionnaire to your workshop facilitator at the next session.

SESSION 7

YOUR ACTION PLAN

Session 7
Goals

GOALS OF SESSION 7

The goals of this session are to help you:

1. Understand the functions of the three components of the action plan sequence:

   a. the strategic plan
   b. the management plan
   c. the operational plan

2. Develop your own action plan for resolving your top priority problem.

Session 7
Workshop Activities

1. Journal Report

    During this group activity, you will discuss your journal entries and any new insights you have gained since the last workshop session.

    Notes:

2. Small Group Discussion: Problem Review

    Directions: Share with your group any new insights you have gained since your last session that might affect your understanding of your problem or its related environmental factors. Are there any changes you would like to make either in your problem statement or list of environmental factors? If so, write them here.

Session 7
Workshop Activities

3. Lecture: Creating Your Action Plan

   This lecture presents a case study as an illustration of how you can create your strategic, management, and operational plans.

   Notes:

Session 7
Workshop Activities

4. Exercise: Identifying Components of the Action Plan

Directions: In front of each example, place the letter of the action plan component it represents. The examples belong to a person whose problem statement is:

"I am dissatisfied with my present job, which is causing me loss of self-esteem and self-profit because of the job's lack of creative opportunities."

Examples

_____ 1. Contact a vocational counselor by June 1st

_____ 2. I want to be more creative.

_____ 3. My present job does not satisfy my creative activity needs; within one month, I will have decided what new creative activities I would like in a job."

_____ 4. Go to library and research career opportunities.

_____ 5. Make a list of areas in which I am most creative.

_____ 6. My present job does not satisfy my creative activity needs; within one year, I want to be working in a new job which promises to satisfy these needs.

_____ 7. Use "help wanted" ads and job placement organizations to find possible new job opportunities.

_____ 8. Finish research of career opportunities by May 1st.

Action Plan Components

a. Strategic plan
b. Management plan
c. Operational plan
d. Not an action plan component

PLEASE CONTINUE ON TO THE NEXT PAGE.

-83-

Session 7
Workshop Activities

_____ 9. Have Jan develop a list of careers she would prefer I pursue.

_____ 10. See a vocational counselor.

5. Follow-up to Exercise

In this group activity, you discuss the correct answers to the exercise. You may wish to make a note of any points made that add to your understanding of the action plans.

Notes:

-84-

Session 7
Workshop Activities

6. My Own Action Plan

Directions: Fill in the planning boxes on this and the next two pages. Base your plan on your top priority problem statement and the environmental factors you have identified. NOTE: Again, write your plans in pencil in case you want to erase and make some changes later on. Then have another workshop participant critique your action plan. "(Additional planning charts for your next onion peeling ventures are included in your kit. More also may be obtained from your workshop facilitator.)"

+--+
| My Strategic Plan |
| |
| |
| |
| |
| |
| |
| |
| |
| |
+--+

PLEASE CONTINUE ON TO THE NEXT PAGE.

Session 7
Workshop Activities

MY MANAGEMENT PLAN

PLEASE CONTINUE ON TO THE NEXT PAGE.

Session 7
Workshop Activities

MY OPERATIONAL PLAN

Session 7
Workshop Activities

7. Constructive Criticism of My Action Plan

    During this activity, you will share your action plan with your fellow workshop participants. Please make a note of any constructive criticism that will help you to improve your plan.

    Notes:

8. Session Summary

    This summary reviews the elements of the action plan and their importance to you.

    Notes:

Session 7
Reading Assignment

SESSION 7: READING ASSIGNMENT

Read the following chapter in the book, <u>Peel Your Own Onion</u>.

<u>CHAPTER 9: Auditing</u>

    Notes:

Session 7
Journal Assignment

SESSION 7: JOURNAL ASSIGNMENT

Directions: Please write your answers to the following questions.

1. I do or do not (circle one) feel my action plan is fairly complete at this point. Explain.

2. Additional things (if any) I should do to complete my action plan are:

3. The point I was at after my life-growth session was:

4. Insights I gained today related to my onion-peeling process are:

5. Things I talked to others about today related to my onion-peeling process are:

6. Today, I'm at this point:

7. I'm ready to try these things:

8. Thoughts on my progress toward self-profit are:

MY EVALUATION OF SESSION 7

Please help us to evaluate the effectiveness of the workshop session in which you just participated by answering the following questions. Then give your completed questionnaire to your workshop facilitator at the next session.

1. Of how much value to you were the activities in this session?

    ____ a. Much value

    ____ b. Some value

    ____ c. Little value

    ____ d. No value

2. Did you increase your self-understanding during this session?

    ____ a. Yes

    ____ b. No

    ____ c. Uncertain

3. Did your confidence in resolving your problems increase as a result of this session?

    ____ a. Yes

    ____ b. No

    ____ c. Uncertain

4. Which activity or activities did you like the most? (You need only write the activity numbers given in the workbook.)

    _____

5. Which activity or activities did you like the least? (Again, just write their activity numbers here.)

    _____

6. Of the activity or activities you liked the least, what would you recommend we do to improve them?

    _____
    _____
    _____
    _____

(Please continue on to the next Page)

7. Was the amount of time spent in discussion during this session satisfactory?

   ____ a. Yes

   ____ b. No, too much time spent in discussion

   ____ c. No, too little time spent in discussion

8. Were there any additional activities you would have liked to participate in during this session? If so, what might they be?

   _____
   _____
   _____
   _____
   _____

Thank you for helping us out! Please remember to give this questionnaire to your workshop facilitator at the next session.

SESSION 8

ANALYZING AND AUDITING YOUR ACTION PLAN

Session 8
Introduction

ANALYZING AND AUDITING YOUR ACTION PLAN

One of the questions I am asked most frequently is "Why do businesses fail?" As a management consultant, I have sought to answer that question numerous times, and the answer is always the same. The primary reason businesses fail is that people fail - fail to analyze their plans and monitor their progress in achieving them! Small businesses especially suffer from this planning oversight. The forgotten plans filed away in bottom desk drawers are legion!

My objective in this session is to help you make sure that never happens to your own personal business, I, Inc. During this session you will explore how to analyze your action plan, particularly in the light of new information that requires a change in your plan. You then will begin the important process of auditing or monitoring your progress toward achieving your plan and resolving your top priority problem.

GOALS OF SESSION 8

The goals of this session are to help you:

1. Understand when and how to analyze your action plan.

2. Understand the technique of auditing.

3. Begin auditing your progress toward resolving your current top priority problem.

Session 8
Workshop Activities

1. Journal Report

    During this group activity, you will discuss your journal entries and any new insights you have gained since the last workshop session.

    Notes:

2. Lecture on Analyzing Your Action Plan

    This lecture explains what analysis is, how it works, and the benefits it offers.

    Notes:

Session 8
Workshop Activities

3. How New Information Might Affect My Action Plan

   Directions: With another workshop participant, discuss how new information may require you to change parts of your plan. The new information might be certain events, changed needs, attitudes, etc.

   Notes:

4. My Expectations for Completing My Action Plan

   Directions: Refer back to your action plan in Section 7 of this book. Rate your expectations for successfully completing each item listed in the action plan boxes on a scale of 0 - 10, with 10 representing your most highest expectation. For example, next to your strategic plan you might write a 9 or 10.

Session 8
Workshop Activities

5. How I Will Audit My Action Plan

   Directions: Write below a schedule for auditing your action plan during the next six months.

6. Session Summary

   This summary reviews the analysis and audit phases of the natural planning sequence.

   Notes:

Session 8
Journal Assignment

SESSION 8: JOURNAL ASSIGNMENT

Directions: Starting today, record your progress in achieving your action plan using the daily progress sheets on the following pages. At the end of each seven-day period, complete the weekly auditing sheet. These forms will help you begin the important process of monitoring your success in achieving your action plan.

Session 8
Daily Progress Sheet

DAILY PROGRESS SHEET

Date:_____

1. Today, I took these steps toward achieving my action plan:

2. Problems (if any) I encountered were:

3. Things I can do to surmount these problems (if any) are:

4. Tomorrow I am prepared to do these things:

5. Arrangements I should make to do these things tomorrow are:

Session 8
Daily Progress Sheet

DAILY PROGRESS SHEET

Date: _____

1. Today, I took these steps toward achieving my action plan:

2. Problems (if any) I encountered were:

3. Things I can do to surmount these problems (if any) are:

4. Tomorrow I am prepared to do these things:

5. Arrangements I should make to do these things tomorrow are:

Session 8
Daily Progress Sheet

DAILY PROGRESS SHEET

Date:_____

1. Today, I took these steps toward achieving my action plan:

2. Problems (if any) I encountered were:

3. Things I can do to surmount these problems (if any) are:

4. Tomorrow I am prepared to do these things:

5. Arrangements I should make to do these things tomorrow are:

Session 8
Daily Progress Sheet

DAILY PROGRESS SHEET

Date:_____

1. Today, I took these steps toward achieving my action plan:

2. Problems (if any) I encountered were:

3. Things I can do to surmount these problems (if any) are:

4. Tomorrow I am prepared to do these things:

5. Arrangements I should make to do these things tomorrow are:

Session 8
Daily Progress Sheet

DAILY PROGRESS SHEET

Date:_____

1. Today, I took these steps toward achieving my action plan:

2. Problems (if any) I encountered were:

3. Things I can do to surmount these problems (if any) are:

4. Tomorrow I am prepared to do these things:

5. Arrangements I should make to do these things tomorrow are:

Session 8
Daily Progress Sheet

DAILY PROGRESS SHEET

Date:_____

1. Today, I took these steps toward achieving my action plan:

2. Problems (if any) I encountered were:

3. Things I can do to surmount these problems (if any) are:

4. Tomorrow I am prepared to do these things:

5. Arrangements I should make to do these things tomorrow are:

Session 8
Daily Progress Sheet

DAILY PROGRESS SHEET

Date:_____

1. Today, I took these steps toward achieving my action plan:

2. Problems (if any) I encountered were:

3. Things I can do to surmount these problems (if any) are:

4. Tomorrow I am prepared to do these things:

5. Arrangements I should make to do these things tomorrow are:

Session 8
Weekly Auditing Sheet

WEEKLY AUDITING SHEET

Date:_____

1. My major accomplishments in following my action plan this week were:

2. Significant problems I encountered were:

3. Problems that remain unresolved are:

4. New Information I learned that affects my action plan is:

5. Adjustments in my plan that I may or will have to make are:

Session 8
Daily Progress Sheet

DAILY PROGRESS SHEET

Date:_____

1. Today, I took these steps toward achieving my action plan:

2. Problems (if any) I encountered were:

3. Things I can do to surmount these problems (if any) are:

4. Tomorrow I am prepared to do these things:

5. Arrangements I should make to do these things tomorrow are:

Session 8
Daily Progress Sheet

DAILY PROGRESS SHEET

Date:_____

1. Today, I took these steps toward achieving my action plan:

2. Problems (if any) I encountered were:

3. Things I can do to surmount these problems (if any) are:

4. Tomorrow I am prepared to do these things:

5. Arrangements I should make to do these things tomorrow are:

Session 8
Daily Progress Sheet

DAILY PROGRESS SHEET

Date:_____

1. Today, I took these steps toward achieving my action plan:

2. Problems (if any) I encountered were:

3. Things I can do to surmount these problems (if any) are:

4. Tomorrow I am prepared to do these things:

5. Arrangements I should make to do these things tomorrow are:

Session 8
Daily Progress Sheet

DAILY PROGRESS SHEET

Date:_____

1. Today, I took these steps toward achieving my action plan:

2. Problems (if any) I encountered were:

3. Things I can do to surmount these problems (if any) are:

4. Tomorrow I am prepared to do these things:

5. Arrangements I should make to do these things tomorrow are:

Session 8
Daily Progress Sheet

DAILY PROGRESS SHEET

Date: _____

1. Today, I took these steps toward achieving my action plan:

2. Problems (if any) I encountered were:

3. Things I can do to surmount these problems (if any) are:

4. Tomorrow I am prepared to do these things:

5. Arrangements I should make to do these things tomorrow are:

Session 8
Daily Progress Sheet

DAILY PROGRESS SHEET

Date:_____

1. Today, I took these steps toward achieving my action plan:

2. Problems (if any) I encountered were:

3. Things I can do to surmount these problems (if any) are:

4. Tomorrow I am prepared to do these things:

5. Arrangements I should make to do these things tomorrow are:

Session 8
Daily Progress Sheet

DAILY PROGRESS SHEET

Date:_____

1. Today, I took these steps toward achieving my action plan:

2. Problems (if any) I encountered were:

3. Things I can do to surmount these problems (if any) are:

4. Tomorrow I am prepared to do these things:

5. Arrangements I should make to do these things tomorrow are:

Session 8
Weekly Auditing Sheet

WEEKLY AUDITING SHEET

Date:_____

1. My major accomplishments in following my action plan this week were:

2. Significant problems I encountered were:

3. Problems that remain unresolved are:

4. New Information I learned that affects my action plan is:

5. Adjustments in my plan that I may or will have to make are:

Session 8
Daily Progress Sheet

DAILY PROGRESS SHEET

Date:_____

1. Today, I took these steps toward achieving my action plan:

2. Problems (if any) I encountered were:

3. Things I can do to surmount these problems (if any) are:

4. Tomorrow I am prepared to do these things:

5. Arrangements I should make to do these things tomorrow are:

Session 8
Daily Progress Sheet

DAILY PROGRESS SHEET

Date:_____

1. Today, I took these steps toward achieving my action plan:

2. Problems (if any) I encountered were:

3. Things I can do to surmount these problems (if any) are:

4. Tomorrow I am prepared to do these things:

5. Arrangements I should make to do these things tomorrow are:

Session 8
Daily Progress Sheet

DAILY PROGRESS SHEET

Date:_____

1. Today, I took these steps toward achieving my action plan:

2. Problems (if any) I encountered were:

3. Things I can do to surmount these problems (if any) are:

4. Tomorrow I am prepared to do these things:

5. Arrangements I should make to do these things tomorrow are:

Session 8
Daily Progress Sheet

DAILY PROGRESS SHEET

Date:_____

1. Today, I took these steps toward achieving my action plan:

2. Problems (if any) I encountered were:

3. Things I can do to surmount these problems (if any) are:

4. Tomorrow I am prepared to do these things:

5. Arrangements I should make to do these things tomorrow are:

Session 8
Daily Progress Sheet

DAILY PROGRESS SHEET

Date:_____

1. Today, I took these steps toward achieving my action plan:

2. Problems (if any) I encountered were:

3. Things I can do to surmount these problems (if any) are:

4. Tomorrow I am prepared to do these things:

5. Arrangements I should make to do these things tomorrow are:

Session 8
Daily Progress Sheet

DAILY PROGRESS SHEET

Date:_____

1. Today, I took these steps toward achieving my action plan:

2. Problems (if any) I encountered were:

3. Things I can do to surmount these problems (if any) are:

4. Tomorrow I am prepared to do these things:

5. Arrangements I should make to do these things tomorrow are:

DAILY PROGRESS SHEET

Date:_____

1. Today, I took these steps toward achieving my action plan:

2. Problems (if any) I encountered were:

3. Things I can do to surmount these problems (if any) are:

4. Tomorrow I am prepared to do these things:

5. Arrangements I should make to do these things tomorrow are:

Session 8
Weekly Auditing Sheet

WEEKLY AUDITING SHEET

Date:_____

1. My major accomplishments in following my action plan this week were:

2. Significant problems I encountered were:

3. Problems that remain unresolved are:

4. New Information I learned that affects my action plan is:

5. Adjustments in my plan that I may or will have to make are:

Session 8
Daily Progress Sheet

DAILY PROGRESS SHEET

Date:_____

1. Today, I took these steps toward achieving my action plan:

2. Problems (if any) I encountered were:

3. Things I can do to surmount these problems (if any) are:

4. Tomorrow I am prepared to do these things:

5. Arrangements I should make to do these things tomorrow are:

Session 8
Daily Progress Sheet

DAILY PROGRESS SHEET

Date:_____

1. Today, I took these steps toward achieving my action plan:

2. Problems (if any) I encountered were:

3. Things I can do to surmount these problems (if any) are:

4. Tomorrow I am prepared to do these things:

5. Arrangements I should make to do these things tomorrow are:

Session 8
Daily Progress Sheet

DAILY PROGRESS SHEET

Date:_____

1. Today, I took these steps toward achieving my action plan:

2. Problems (if any) I encountered were:

3. Things I can do to surmount these problems (if any) are:

4. Tomorrow I am prepared to do these things:

5. Arrangements I should make to do these things tomorrow are:

Session 8
Daily Progress Sheet

DAILY PROGRESS SHEET

Date:_____

1. Today, I took these steps toward achieving my action plan:

2. Problems (if any) I encountered were:

3. Things I can do to surmount these problems (if any) are:

4. Tomorrow I am prepared to do these things:

5. Arrangements I should make to do these things tomorrow are:

Session 8
Daily Progress Sheet

DAILY PROGRESS SHEET

Date:_____

1. Today, I took these steps toward achieving my action plan:

2. Problems (if any) I encountered were:

3. Things I can do to surmount these problems (if any) are:

4. Tomorrow I am prepared to do these things:

5. Arrangements I should make to do these things tomorrow are:

Session 8
Daily Progress Sheet

DAILY PROGRESS SHEET

Date:_____

1. Today, I took these steps toward achieving my action plan:

2. Problems (if any) I encountered were:

3. Things I can do to surmount these problems (if any) are:

4. Tomorrow I am prepared to do these things:

5. Arrangements I should make to do these things tomorrow are:

Session 8
Daily Progress Sheet

DAILY PROGRESS SHEET

Date:_____

1. Today, I took these steps toward achieving my action plan:

2. Problems (if any) I encountered were:

3. Things I can do to surmount these problems (if any) are:

4. Tomorrow I am prepared to do these things:

5. Arrangements I should make to do these things tomorrow are:

Session 8
Weekly Auditing Sheet

WEEKLY AUDITING SHEET

Date:_____

1. My major accomplishments in following my action plan this week were:

2. Significant problems I encountered were:

3. Problems that remain unresolved are:

4. New Information I learned that affects my action plan is:

5. Adjustments in my plan that I may or will have to make are:

MY EVALUATION OF SESSION 8

Please help us to evaluate the effectiveness of the workshop session in which you just participated by answering the following questions. Then give your completed questionnaire to your workshop facilitator at the next session.

1. Of how much value to you were the activities in this session?

    ____ a. Much value

    ____ b. Some value

    ____ c. Little value

    ____ d. No value

2. Did you increase your self-understanding during this session?

    ____ a. Yes

    ____ b. No

    ____ c. Uncertain

3. Did your confidence in resolving your problems increase as a result of this session?

    ____ a. Yes

    ____ b. No

    ____ c. Uncertain

4. Which activity or activities did you like the most? (You need only write the activity numbers given in the workbook.)

    _____

5. Which activity or activities did you like the least? (Again, just write their activity numbers here.)

    _____

6. Of the activity or activities you liked the least, what would you recommend we do to improve them?

    _____

    _____

    _____

    _____

(Please continue on to the next Page)

7. Was the amount of time spent in discussion during this session satisfactory?

   ____ a. Yes

   ____ b. No, too much time spent in discussion

   ____ c. No, too little time spent in discussion

8. Were there any additional activities you would have liked to participate in during this session? If so, what might they be?

   _____
   _____
   _____
   _____
   _____

Thank you for helping us out! Please remember to give this questionnaire to your workshop facilitator at the next session.

SESSION 9

THE ONION PEELERS CONVENTION

Session 9
Introduction

THE ONION PEELERS CONVENTION

When I first began conducting this workshop, I found that one of its most satisfying outcomes was the friendships that developed and the interest and concern of the workshop participants in each others' progress toward achieving their action plans. As a result, I developed a follow-up session to the workshop in which everyone can come together and affirm their accomplishments in peeling their own onions.

I call this follow-up session "The Onion Peelers Convention" because it is primarily a time for you to meet informally with your fellow onion peelers and compare notes on your onion-peeling accomplishments, problems encountered along the way, and adjustments you have had to make. You will find that some onion peelers have experienced major life changes since you saw them last. Others will have made significant strides toward accomplishing their action plans. Most importantly, you will find that you too have made progress towards achieving your own plan and that sharing and affirming your progress with your fellow onion peelers will motivate you even more to follow through with your plan!

So, welcome to The Onion Peelers Convention! Let's explore our progress in the fine art of onion-peeling!

Session 9
Goals

GOALS OF SESSION 9

The goals of this session are to help you:

1. Evaluate your progress in achieving your action plan for your first onion peeling project.

2. Affirm your commitment to following your action plan.

Session 9
Workshop Activities

1. My Progress In Onion-Peeling

    Throughout this session, you will be discussing your progress on your first onion peeling project. You may wish to make a note of any new insights you gained today about your top priority problem, your accomplishments so far, and any adjustments you may have to make.

    Notes:

PEELING MORE LAYERS

You have begun your first onion peeling project and by now have made some real progress toward achieving your action plan and resolving your top priority problem. The question now is when do you start peeling more layers? Now? Or later on when you have successfully resolved your first problem?

That really is a question only you can answer! After all, as chief executive officer of I, Inc., you and you alone are in the best position to consider when to undertake new onion peeling ventures and what they should be! But there are some questions I would like to leave you with that I have found helpful in asking myself before starting to peel more layers of my onion. Here they are:

1. "Have I checked my Aha! Chart?"

    When I check my Aha! Chart periodically, I can see where I am at now in terms of satisfying my needs. I become aware of new need areas and problems that inhibit my growth. Most importantly, I can get a better sense of what <u>pressing</u> problems exist that demand my attention.

2. "Does the problem I just resolved (or the problem I am still working on now) change my perspective?"

    Very often, solving one problem affects my perspective on my other problems and unmet needs. Some issues I thought pretty major disappear, while new ones come to the forefront- sometimes quite unexpectedly!

3. "Have my priorities changed?"

    When I reconsider my problems and use the pairing method to prioritize them, I can see if another problem has assumed top priority. Then I can decide if it is pressing enough to take action on it now.

4. "If I already am peeling one onion layer now, can I afford to peel another?"

    I use that word "afford" quite deliberately, because when I choose to undertake two onion peeling projects, I know I must be able to afford the extra time, energy and sheer concentration it requires to work effectively on both at the same time. I don't want to jeopardize one because of the other!

> Sometimes I feel I can commit myself to handling two major
> problems simultaneously. Other times I find I can only
> deal with my big top priority problem and perhaps a single
> lesser one. It all depends on my life situation at that
> time.

Life rarely allows you the opportunity to deal with your problems one at a time. But it is important that you take care in selecting the problems you most need to deal with now as you seek to free yourself of the things that inhibit your personal growth. Gradually, you will become more skilled in this business of peeling onions, moving along your scale of needs towards the ultimate goal of self-profit or self-actualization. You have just made an excellent start, and now I wish you the best of luck in your future onion peeling!

MY EVALUATION OF SESSION 9

Please help us to evaluate the effectiveness of the workshop session in which you just participated by answering the following questions. Then give your completed questionnaire to your workshop facilitator at the next session.

1. Of how much value to you were the activities in this session?

    ____ a. Much value

    ____ b. Some value

    ____ c. Little value

    ____ d. No value

2. Did you increase your self-understanding during this session?

    ____ a. Yes

    ____ b. No

    ____ c. Uncertain

3. Did your confidence in resolving your problems increase as a result of this session?

    ____ a. Yes

    ____ b. No

    ____ c. Uncertain

4. Which activity or activities did you like the most? (You need only write the activity numbers given in the workbook.)

    _____

5. Which activity or activities did you like the least? (Again, just write their activity numbers here.)

    _____

6. Of the activity or activities you liked the least, what would you recommend we do to improve them?

    _____
    _____
    _____
    _____

(Please continue on to the next Page)

7. Was the amount of time spent in discussion during this session satisfactory?

   ____ a. Yes

   ____ b. No, too much time spent in discussion

   ____ c. No, too little time spent in discussion

8. Were there any additional activities you would have liked to participate in during this session? If so, what might they be?

   _____
   _____
   _____
   _____
   _____

Thank you for helping us out! Please remember to give this questionnaire to your workshop facilitator at the next session.